Animals
as
Parents

Animals
as
Parents

Millicent E. Selsam

illustrated by John Kaufmann

William Morrow and Company
New York 1965

The author wishes to thank
KENNETH COOPER
associated with the
Department of Animal Behavior,
Museum of Natural History,
New York City,
for reading the
manuscript of this book.

Contents

Animals
as
Parents

Introduction

What are animals like as parents? Do all animals take care of their young ones? Do birds love their baby birds? What happens if you take a newborn lamb away from its mother for a while? Can monkey babies be raised by artificial mothers?

All of these questions and many more have been asked and answered by scientists specializing in the field of animal behavior. They find the answers to their questions in two ways. One is by watching animals in their natural surroundings. The other is by experimenting with them, either where they live or in a laboratory.

Careful observation of the behavior of animals can reveal a great deal. Scientists have followed monkeys and apes through forests watching them and keeping notes. They take photographs, moving pictures, and sound recordings. From such work we have learned much about the way baby monkeys and apes are brought up in the wild. Other scientists have spent hours, days, and weeks watching a few birds bring up their young ones, or watching great colonies of them on vast breeding grounds. Still others have observed herds of animals as they grazed and rested on the plain.

TWO METHODS OF OBSERVING ANIMALS

watching from a blind   following in a jeep

The observer may spend a long time letting the animals get used to him, so that they will go about their normal activities undisturbed. He may sit quietly in a blind—a simple little tent or windbreak with a hole in it through which he can watch the animals. Sometimes he may sit in a tree, or follow the animals on horseback or in a jeep.

Anyone who observes a limited number of a particular kind of animal soon learns to distinguish them, for no two animals look exactly alike once one gets to know them. But when observing large numbers of animals, some kind of marking becomes necessary. Usually the observer attaches little plastic or metal tags to a part of the animal.

Sometimes, instead of following the animals or watching them where they live, the scientist brings a bit of their natural environment into the laboratory. Fish can live in aquaria, and scientists have learned much about them as parents by using aquaria to observe them indoors. They have watched porpoises in huge outdoor tanks. Through portholes in these tanks, they have seen what goes on underwater when a baby porpoise is born.

Observing animals usually gives rise to many questions which can only be answered by experimentation. The scientists who have watched monkeys and apes in their natural surroundings have noticed how well monkey mothers take care of their babies. But what factors enter into this infant-mother relationship? What happens when baby monkeys are separated from their mothers and provided with food? Do they grow up to be normal monkeys? Or do they need more than food from the mother? In the laboratory, experiments can reveal exactly what enters into the relationship between monkey mothers and their young.

It is easy to make mistakes when interpreting what animals are doing. It is hard to keep remembering that animals live in a different kind of world from our own. They see, hear, smell, and taste things differently. And they do not have human intelligence or emotions, so we must avoid interpreting their behavior in terms of our own feelings and thoughts. For example, it looks to us as though parent birds are devoted to their young in the same way that human parents are devoted to theirs. But only experimental work can show whether this interpretation is true.

There are as many different ways of caring for the young as there are different animals. Chapter one will give a glimpse of the overall pattern of parental behavior among animals. The rest of the book is devoted to parental care among birds and mammals, for most of the new experimental and field work has been done by scientists with these two groups of animals.

One

The
Ways
of
Animal
Parents

In order that animals survive for generation after generation after generation, at least two offspring from each pair of animal parents must grow to adult size and breed again. If only two survive, the population stays the same. If more than two survive, the population increases. If less than two survive, the animal will gradually vanish from the face of the earth. However, there are different ways of maintaining the necessary balance for survival.

Most animals of the sea broadcast their eggs into a watery

17

world and provide no parental care at all. But these animals survive because they produce immense numbers of eggs. Millions upon millions of eggs of oysters, clams, snails, sea worms, starfish, jellyfish, and fish float on the surface of the sea. A single oyster may release more than five hundred million eggs a season. A single codfish can lay six and a half million eggs every year. If all of them changed into oysters or codfish and grew to adult size, the oceans would

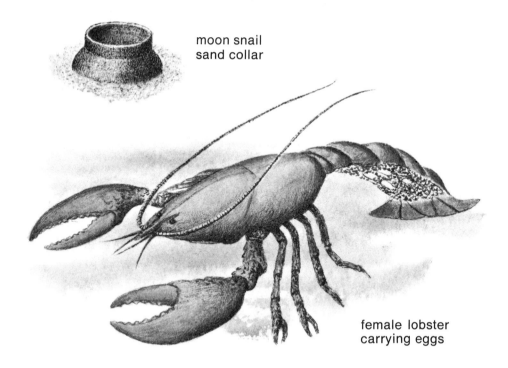

moon snail
sand collar

female lobster
carrying eggs

soon be teeming with these animals. But the eggs and the young that hatch from these eggs usually land inside another sea animal bigger than themselves. Or they may be tossed upon the shore by storms, drift into water that is too warm or too cold for them, or be caught and collected by people for food. The hazards are great. Despite them, codfish and oysters remain in the world, because the enormous number of eggs and young are enough to counteract these losses.

Some sea animals produce a smaller number of eggs, but provide a little protection for them. The marine moon snail pushes a jellylike sheet of eggs around its smooth globe of a shell. The eggs pick up a thin layer of sand on either side, and the newly formed sand collar hardens and holds its shape when the snail moves on. If you find one of these sand collars and hold it up to the light, you will see the tiny eggs clear as glass scattered through the inside layer of the egg case.

Large-sized sea snails called whelks produce long strings of parchmentlike bags. Each bag contains about three dozen eggs, which develop into tiny whelks. When a pore in the bag opens, the whelks, complete with shells, emerge.

The female lobster and some crabs carry their eggs and young around with them attached to their swimming legs or their abdomen.

Fish as Parents

Most common ocean fish scatter their millions of eggs into the sea and give them no care. Many of the fish that live in the more protected waters of bays and inlets, and in freshwater lakes and streams, however, lay fewer eggs and take care of them in some ways. They may build nests, and some may then guard the eggs until they hatch. A few carry their eggs in their mouth until they are developed. When the eggs hatch, the young may stay with the parent for a time. Some kinds of fish retain the eggs inside their body and bear live young.

The female brook trout is an example of a fish that makes a nest for its eggs and does no more. The male sunfish makes shallow, round nests in the sand close to shore. After the female deposits eggs in the nests the male stays around and defends the eggs from predators. He may even watch over the newly hatched young for a short time.

Both male and female catfish choose a natural sheltered hollow as a nest, and then keep the developing eggs well ventilated by paddling their bottom fin against the eggs and tumbling them about. When the eggs hatch they form a little school of coal-black fish. Then the parent fish herd them around, keeping the young ones in a compact group by swimming around them in circles. This herding goes on till

20

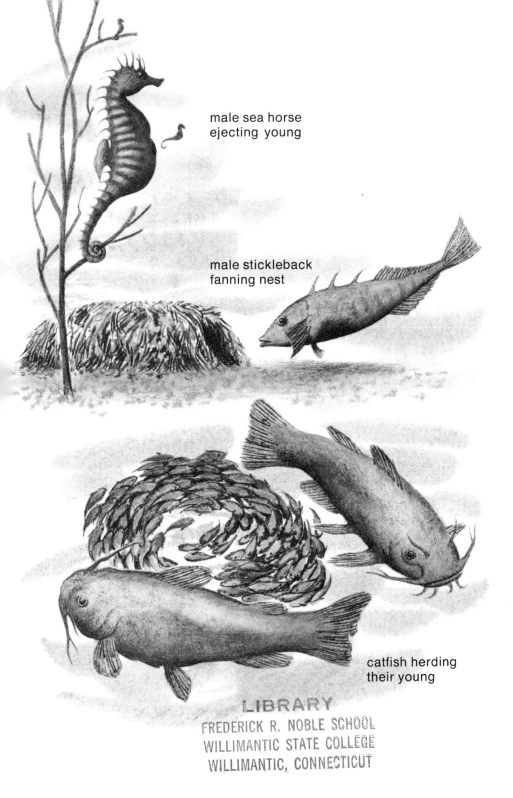

male sea horse
ejecting young

male stickleback
fanning nest

catfish herding
their young

the little fish have reached a length of almost two inches.

Sticklebacks build nests of waterweeds. The male alone takes care of the eggs, ventilating them by fanning water through the nest with movements of his fins. Experiments were done to find out what made him fan his fins at certain times. The results showed that the male stickleback responds to the oxygen content in the water over the eggs. If the oxygen content of the nest water was lowered artificially, the male started to fan. This response is automatic. He does not know what he is doing. After about a week the eggs hatch. The male tears the nest open, but the young remain in what is left of it for a few days. Then they start to swim out. The male chases after them, trying to catch them. He sucks them into his mouth, then spits them back into the nest area. After another week he stops this activity and the young sticklebacks go their own way.

Sea catfish carry parental care a step farther. The female transfers her eggs into the male's mouth, and he keeps them there for a whole month while they are developing. Each egg is about as big as a marble, and he usually carries between ten and thirty eggs at a time. The eggs hatch and the father continues to hold the young fish in his mouth for a few more weeks. When the young fish are about two inches long, they leave the parent's mouth for good. During the entire period that the male takes care of the eggs and young, he eats no food.

Other mouthbreeding types of fish carry their young in their mouth while they are developing. Then, for a while after that, the young rush into the parent's mouth in times of danger. The tilapia, a perchlike fish that breeds in tropical

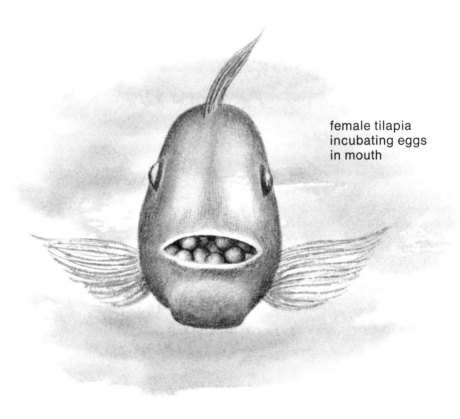

female tilapia
incubating eggs
in mouth

rivers and lakes, shows such behavior. There are many kinds of tilapias; among some the male fish cares for the young and among others the female does.

The female *Tilapia natalensis* (Tilapia is the name of the genus and *natalensis* the name of the species) snaps up several hundred fertilized eggs into her mouth. During the period while they are developing, she eats no food. The eggs take about twelve days to hatch, and then are ejected from her mouth. The young form a school and follow the mother fish. When some big object approaches or there are sudden turbulent currents in the water, the female makes violent swimming movements with her fins and retreats toward her young, swimming in a diagonal position with her head down. The young respond to this action by swimming toward her and swarming around her. They particularly gather around her head, near her eyes, and the dark corners at the base of her fins, hanging there like tassels till they manage to enter her open mouth.

Experiments have shown that the disturbance in the water made by the mother fish's calling movements is what makes the young fish move toward her. The female was put into a tank right next to the tank of the young fish. They could see her, but they did not respond when she made these movements. When the water in their tank was disturbed, however, the young fish approached and swarmed against the glass in front of the female's head.

When the danger is very great, the female *Tilapia natalensis* does not take the young into her mouth, but first attacks the intruder biting, butting and beating her tail. The young fish scatter toward the bottom of the tank as she makes such movements. After the intruder leaves, the female goes to the young, makes her calling movements, and snaps them up into her mouth.

At the end of four to five days the female no longer takes the young into her mouth. Parental care is over, and the young fish are on their own.

Sometimes eggs develop in special brood pouches. The female sea horse, for example, places the eggs inside the pouch of the male. The tissue of the pouch turns into a network of spongy compartments full of blood vessels. One egg settles in each compartment, and nourishment passes from the blood in the vessels to the eggs. When the young are fully developed, the pouch opens. Father sea horse takes hold of a bit of seaweed with his tail, and then contractions of his muscles shoot the baby fish out through the opening in the pouch.

A few kinds of fish give birth to live young. Sharks are one example, and they usually have from 1 to 20 young, depending on the species. Guppies, which many people keep as pets in aquaria, bear up to 126 young.

It is known that guppies and some other fish will eat their young if they have the opportunity. Many others do not, however, and it is interesting to find out why. Several experiments with jewel fish have been done with this question in mind. Jewel-fish parents stay with their eggs, protect them, and aerate them. After the eggs hatch, the school of young follow their parents for about two weeks. In place of their own eggs, the experimenter put eggs of another species. When they hatched, the parents accepted and raised the strange young. If they came across eggs of their own species, they ate them. The next time these same fish bred, they were allowed to keep their own eggs. They ate them too. They had become conditioned to the adopted type of eggs and young.

Another scientist repeated this experiment and got different results. In his experiment the jewel-fish parents raised their own eggs, then raised foreign eggs, and even took care of mixed schools of young. This scientist claims that the important factor is the stage of the parents' brooding activity. In the first stage the parents will accept only eggs. Later they accept tiny young fish just hatched. And still later they accept older fish. The eggs of young must match the brooding stage of the parent in order to be accepted. Further research will have to be done before we know which experiment is more accurate.

Even those parents that do not eat their eggs and young generally will come to a point where their behavior changes. Eventually parental activity vanishes, and the young fish may be eaten later by the very mother who tended it so carefully.

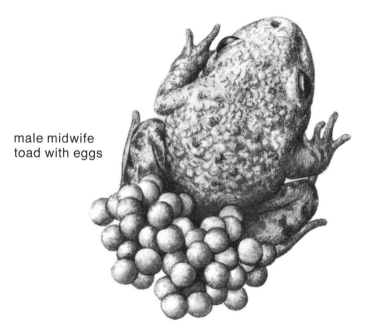

male midwife
toad with eggs

Frogs and Toads as Parents

Most frogs and toads lay their eggs in a pond and desert them. The tadpoles hatch out, and no parent looks after them. They may be eaten by fish, ducks, or other animals. A few manage to survive.

But there are always exceptions. A few kinds of frogs and toads not native to this country do care for their eggs. The male midwife toad found in western Europe wraps its long strings of eggs around its hind legs and retires to a damp place till the eggs develop. Some frog eggs change into tadpoles and grow in special chambers, or pits, in the body of the parent. Some South American frogs build a watery nursery for their eggs. They live in trees and lay their eggs in holes that they first waterproof by lining them with wax taken from the nests of bees. Rainwater then collects in the holes and the eggs change into tadpoles in the tiny artificial pools.

Reptiles as Parents

Of the thousands of species of reptiles, only a few kinds of snakes and a few kinds of alligators and crocodiles care for their young. The others pick a place in which to lay their eggs and desert them. Snakes may lay eggs in hollow logs, in manure piles, in sand, under the litter of the forest floor, or in the muddy banks of streams. Although most of them leave the eggs, a few snakes remain coiled around them and stay near till they hatch. There are also quite a number of snakes that retain the eggs inside their body and give birth to live young.

Alligators give their young the most care among the reptiles. The American alligator scrapes together a pile of vegetation and mud, and then digs a cavity on top of it. Fifteen to eighty eggs are deposited in the cavity and covered. The female alligator guards the nest. When the young babies are about to hatch they make grunting sounds that act as a stimulus to the female, who responds by tearing open the top of the mound. The young alligators then push their way through the loose covering and run to the female at the edge of the water, *umph, umph, umphing* all the time. Until the following spring the young alligators stay together and are protected by their big mother. Then they scatter to live their own life.

Birds and Mammals as Parents

Two large groups of animals, the birds and mammals, have developed parental care to higher levels than any other members of the animal kingdom. Birds lay eggs and take great care of them and the young that hatch from them until they are independent. The mammals carry their young inside their body where they develop until they are born alive, and then one or both parents take care of the newly born young ones.

snake hatching from egg

alligator on nest

Two

Birds' Nests and Eggs

Not long ago I watched a mother catbird sitting on her eggs in a nest. A few minutes later she flew off and I saw four blue eggs. Ten minutes later the mother bird was back. How long would it take before the eggs hatched out? Did the mother catbird learn how to build a nest or did this ability come automatically? Did she always lay just four eggs? What did the male bird have to do with the care of the eggs? These questions arose in my mind, and I found later that many scientists before me had asked similar

33

questions about the catbird as well as many other kinds of birds.

From scientific observations we know that the female catbird takes seven days to make her nest. She does most of the work, but the male bird, or father-to-be, brings nesting material. Three days go by after the nest is completed. Then the first egg is laid. Each day the mother catbird lays another egg. When the third egg is laid, she begins to incubate, or sit on, her eggs. In the meantime, a special part of her abdominal skin has lost its feathers and the blood vessels there have enlarged. Through this brood patch heat is easily transferred to the eggs. After the fourth egg is laid, the mother catbird sits on her eggs for twelve days more. She alone attends the eggs, but the father catbird stays around the nest area and sings loudly every once in a while. This behavior helps to keep other catbirds away. After thirteen days the eggs hatch out and four baby catbirds are in the nest.

The Nest

What makes the mother catbird start to build a nest? Does she know to what use the nest will be put? We have learned from experiments that certain chemical substances in the blood, called hormones, are responsible for the way

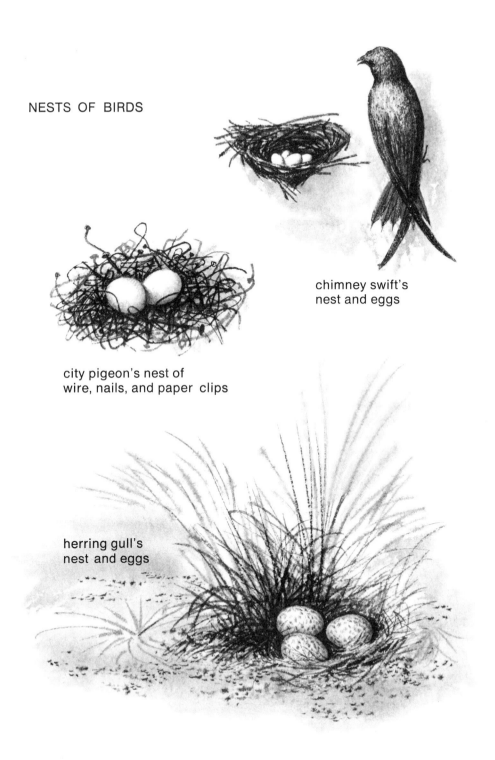

NESTS OF BIRDS

chimney swift's
nest and eggs

city pigeon's nest of
wire, nails, and paper clips

herring gull's
nest and eggs

birds act in the spring. The longer daylight affects the pituitary gland at the base of a bird's brain. This gland produces hormones that go through the blood to the reproductive organs and make the bird ready to breed and build nests. Actually the bird has no idea that she is preparing a nest for her eggs and young. She is merely going through a set of automatic actions in response to the hormones in her blood. Early in the spring season an egg, even a gull's egg, is food to a gull. But when the hormones are produced later in the season, the bird sits on the egg and does not eat it, unless an accident happens. If a gull egg is cracked open, the gull mother eats the egg even while she is sitting on other uncracked eggs in the nest.

The typical bird's nest to most of us is round, open on top, has coarse material on the outside and softer stuff lining the inside. But a nest may be a mere layer of pine needles, a tunnel in a sandy cliff, a hole in a tree, or a fancy hanging basket. Nests vary a great deal, and experts can look at one and tell you the name of the bird that made it. Certain birds always use sticks, others feathers, special grasses, mud, or combinations of these things. Some birds use whatever is handy—from pieces of wool dropped on a porch to nails, wires, and paper clips.

Experiments show that birds can build the very first nest

as well as the last. No previous experience is necessary. Evidently birds are born able to build nests like the ones their parents built before them. Canaries have been raised in captivity for many generations without ever having a chance to see a canary's nest. Yet if they are given suitable material, they build a typical canary's nest.

The Number of Eggs

Does a bird always lay a certain number of eggs? If you look this question up in bird books, you will find it does. The books give the usual or average number of eggs different birds lay. The catbird usually lays four. Pigeons lay two, an emperor penguin one, while a duck lays up to sixteen.

Some birds lay the same number of eggs even if the eggs are removed one by one from the nest as they appear. The bird then may move on and build a second nest when her eggs are gone, sometimes even a third or fourth nest, and lay the usual number of eggs typical of her kind in each nest. But other birds can be tricked into laying many more eggs than normal in the same nest. In one famous experiment, eggs were removed from a flicker (woodpecker) as she laid them. She ended up laying seventy-one eggs in seventy-three days! Our egg-laying chickens are induced in this way to lay an egg almost every day of the year.

catbird
and
hatchlings

snowy owl hatchlings

Incubating the Eggs

The catbird starts to sit on her eggs after the third egg of the four is laid. This pattern is very common among birds. Many of them start to incubate when the last or next to last egg is laid. And that is why if you look into a bird's nest after the eggs are hatched, you see baby birds of about the same size.

The mallard duck lays about ten eggs. Every day the

female lays another egg; she does not sit on her eggs until the last one is laid. The other eggs do not start to develop until the mother duck incubates them, so they all hatch out within hours of each other after about twenty-six days.

But owls begin to incubate their eggs when they lay their first one. Every day or two another egg is added. The first egg hatches out before the others, the second before the third, and so on. If you look into an owl's nest at the right time you can find little owls of different sizes.

While they are being incubated the eggs are turned every once in a while. This movement keeps them evenly warm and prevents the membranes inside from sticking to the shell. The eggs do not have to be covered all of the time. Most small songbirds stay on the eggs for about twenty to thirty minutes, and then fly off for food and spend eight to ten minutes taking care of their own needs.

In many cases the female alone does all the incubating of the eggs, but the male stays around the nest area. The male song sparrow flies to a point near the nest and sings a special loud and sudden song, which is a signal to the female to leave the nest for her off period. The male guards the nest while she is away, but joins her just before she goes back.

Other birds share the incubating of the eggs. Male and

female take turns so that the eggs are covered and kept warm all the time. Each may spend a short period on the nest with changeovers from one partner to the other every ten to twenty minutes. Or there may be regular shifts. Herring gulls relieve each other every few hours. Male pigeons sit on the eggs from 10 A.M. to 4 P.M.; the female takes over at that time and sits through the night. Male Adelie penguins incubate their eggs for two weeks until the female returns for the changeover. Then the nest reliefs become more frequent until they are only three to four days apart at hatching time. The big male emperor penguin of the antarctic regions does all of the incubating. After the female lays her single egg she takes to the sea, and the male incubates the egg for two whole months!

When there are changeovers from one partner to another, there may be nest-relief ceremonies. When one of a mated pair of herons returns to the nest to take a turn on the eggs, the sitting bird rises, and both raise their crest and make loud noises. The brown pelican points its great bill to the sky and advances slowly, waving its head from side to side. The ceremony may involve wing lifting, bowing, calling, or offering nest material. The end result is that the sitting bird steps off the nest and the partner takes its place. Sometimes the arriving bird goes through all the right signals and yet the sitting bird lingers. In this case you may see the relieving bird actually shove the other off the nest.

heron nest relief ceremony

Recognizing the Eggs

Much work has been done to try to find out whether parent birds recognize their own eggs. The results vary with the kind of bird. In a series of tests with herring gulls, it was shown that the gulls could not distinguish their own eggs from other gull eggs. If they were presented with brightly painted wooden eggs, the gulls accepted them as well as their own. Using the wooden eggs, experiments were done to find out whether the size, the shape, or the color made them acceptable to the gulls. The important factor was found to be the round shape. The gulls always selected round models in preference to rectangular-shaped ones. Color did not matter too much, except that red was less attractive than other colors. Also a larger-sized egg stimulated the gulls much more than a small-sized one.

Some birds will sit on anything if it is in the right place. Even stones and light bulbs are accepted by them. Yet there are certain birds, like the Atlantic murres, that *can* distinguish their own eggs from their neighbors'. These birds lay their eggs very close together on rocky ledges. Eggs of three different birds sitting near each other were exchanged. When the birds returned each rolled its own egg back to its original place.

We can tell that many songbirds do not recognize their own eggs, because they accept strange eggs laid in their nest. A song sparrow, for example, will accept the egg of a cowbird laid in its nest. Cowbird females do not incubate their own eggs, but select another bird's nest, wait for the sitting bird to depart, then dash in and lay an egg. The sparrow does not seem to sense the difference between her own eggs and the strange one. She incubates it along with her own and later feeds the young bird along with her own. A tiny little sparrow can often be seen stuffing food into the mouth of a cowbird twice as big as itself.

catbird throwing
out cowbird eggs

sparrow feeding
young cowbird

But even among songbirds there are some that will not accept strange eggs. The catbird throws the strange cowbird egg out of its nest. Yellow warblers have been known to build a new nest over the old one if cowbird eggs have been laid in it.

Eggs may be incubated anywhere from one to eight weeks, depending on the kind of bird. For all, the time finally comes when the baby birds, developing inside the shell, crack the egg. After a few hours or days they manage to get out of it altogether and step out into the world.

44

Three

Birds
as
Parents

Ducklings and chicks hatch out of their egg and in a few hours are fluffy balls of downy soft feathers that can follow their mother. They can walk, run, and, if they are ducks, they can swim too. They can pick up their own food. These birds are typical of a whole group of birds whose young hatch out in an advanced state. They are generally birds that nest on the ground.

Other birds hatch out naked of feathers, blind and weak, and stay helpless in the nest for days or weeks. They have to be fed by the parents constantly. A young song sparrow just begins to open its eyes when it is three days old. It takes eight days for it to get a complete covering of feathers. After ten days of being cared for in the nest, it leaves and wanders in the bushes nearby and the parents keep feeding it until it is a month old.

Ready to Follow

But even the ground-nesting birds that hatch out in an advanced state get warmth and protection from the mother for some time. She also leads them to food. The first thing the young do is to follow their mother. Scientists have asked the question, "What makes a chick or a duckling or gosling follow its mother?"

A famous Austrian biologist, Dr. Konrad Lorenz, showed that geese follow the first moving object they see after they hatch. Usually this object is their mother. But if they see another moving object, they follow it instead. In this case, they first saw the experimenter, Dr. Lorenz, so they followed him. They followed him on land and swam after him in the water. As far as these geese were concerned, he was their mother.

Other ground-nesting birds behave this way too. They follow the first moving object they come into contact with after hatching. This following response is called *imprinting,*

duckling following moving decoy

ducklings following hen

for it imprints on the bird a strong early habit of following its own species. But these birds can also be imprinted easily to other species, so that strange families result. Besides being made to follow human beings, ducks and turkeys have been made to follow hens. In one experiment duck eggs were placed under one hen, and turkey eggs were placed under another. When the eggs hatched, the ducklings followed *their* hen mother, and the turkey poults followed theirs. The young, too, were fully adopted by the mother hens, which chased and pecked at any other young ones even if they were chicks.

Ducks, geese, turkeys, and chicks can be made to follow even inaminate objects. These objects may vary from mechanically moving birds to little boxes pulled back and forth. The response is stronger if the moving object gives off soft, low-pitched sounds repeated at a rapid rate. Dr. Lorenz found that he had to quack like a mother mallard duck in order to make mallard ducklings run after him. He also had to squat low in the grass, for they did not seem to notice him when he was standing up. It was a difficult experiment for Dr. Lorenz, who had to drag himself along squatting and quacking for hours to test the following responses of these ducks.

Other experiments have also shown that sound plays a part

in a chick's ability to recognize its mother. If a sitting hen is removed in the dark from her chicks and another hen placed there instead, the chicks find their own mother by the sounds she makes. In the same way, if different broods of chicks are put together in the dark, the chicks sort themselves out and go to their own mother.

The mother hens, too, recognize their own chicks by sound. If a chick is hidden from the hen, she will find it when it gives a distress call. If the chick is covered with a glass jar and its peeps cannot be heard, the hen takes no notice of it even though she can see the chick.

Turkey mothers will attack dummy young that look exactly right but are silent. If the dummies have speakers that emit the recorded peeps of young turkeys, the hens do not attack. So sound signals play a role in the recognition of the young.

Herring gulls nest in vast colonies and each pair of breeding gulls has a small territory around its nest and young. Gull chicks are everywhere. Does each mother gull know her own chick? Observers watching such colonies of herring gulls report that they have seen gull chicks cross over into the territory of neighboring gulls and be pecked and often killed. Experiments were then planned to find out whether gull parents really did recognize their own chicks. One-day-old grayish downy speckled chicks of different parents were exchanged. In all cases the young were accepted. But the same chicks were attacked when they were exchanged four days later. So we know now that parent gulls learn to distinguish their own young during the first few days after hatching; and after that they take care of only their own. Other experiments show that sound is important for gulls too. The parent gulls respond to the call of their own chicks, even when they cannot see them, while they do not respond to the calls of strange chicks.

Helpless in the Nest

Tree-nesting birds whose young stay in the nest for some time after hatching do not seem to recognize their own young. These young birds can be transferred from one nest to another, and the parents will accept the strange birds. They do not even have to be the same age. The parent birds seem to be more attached to their nests than to their young. If nestlings fall outside the nest, the parents do not recognize them, but fly back to the nest and sit there letting the young ones outside die from lack of food.

A robin will shade an empty nest from the sun while the young lie in a bowl right next to her. This behavior was seen when young robins were taken out of a nest to be

female robin shading
empty nest

weighed in a bowl. The bowl had been put back close to
the nest when the female appeared and spread her wings
over the empty nest, completely indifferent to her young ones
in the bowl beside her.

Food and Feeding

Six minutes after emerging from its shell, a baby robin
was seen "begging" for food. It raised its head and opened
its mouth, or gaped. It also made little peeping sounds. It
is born with this ability to open its mouth wide and cry
at the approach of its parent. A slight shake of the branches
and all heads in the nest go up. When the mouths open they
reveal brilliant colors that help the parent bird direct the
food to the right place. A week later, when these same birds

52

have their eyes open, they only gape when they see the parent or hear it call.

Who gets the most food? Usually there are several birds in the nest, and all their mouths are open wide. The mother or sometimes the father bird simply puts food into the mouth of the bird that gapes the widest, and stretches up higher than the others, and utters the loudest begging notes. The parent bird continues to feed this bird until the nestling, full of food, falls back and refuses to swallow. Food that is not swallowed is picked up out of the mouth of one and offered to the next mouth gaping the widest.

Where there are large broods of young birds, the parents bring food more often than they do to small broods. The actual number of young ones in the nest is not the important stimulus to the parents, however. What is more important is how the nestlings act. If an experimenter keeps replacing well-fed birds in the nest with hungry ones, the gaping and crying of the young birds begging for food causes the parents to bring more.

Is it the gaping or the crying of the young birds that makes the parents respond? In one experiment six hungry birds were hidden in one side of a box and only one bird was left visible in the other side of the box. The calls of the six hungry hidden young ones kept the parents bringing

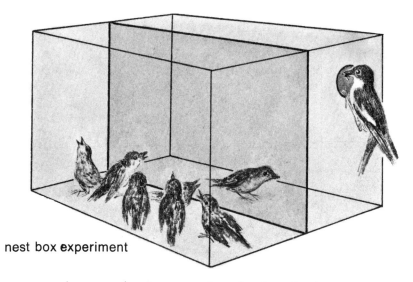

nest box experiment

more and more food, even though the single young one could hardly open its mouth.

The young of ground-nesting birds feed in different ways. Chickens follow the parent bird and pick up food from the ground. *Kuk-kuk-kuk-kuk,* calls the hen, and the chicks come running for food. The mother duck leads her young ones from the nest to a pond or lake, and there her ducklings feed on insects or plants. Gulls regurgitate food in front of their young chicks, then pick up a small piece in the bill tip and present it to them. The chick pecks at the parent's bill tip and gets the food. The bill of the herring gull is yellow with a bright red spot at the tip of the lower bill. Experiments with painted cardboard models have shown

gull chick
being fed

baby robins
being fed

that a young herring gull will peck at the color red more often than at other colors.

The kind of food brought to the nest depends on the kind of bird. The tree-nesting birds usually bring insects like caterpillars, grasshoppers, crickets, softened seeds, or fruits. Gulls eat fish, crabs, and worms, regurgitating the food in softened form for the chicks. Penguin and pelican young put their bill right into the gullet of their parents and feed on shrimp and fish the parents have there. Pigeons regurgitate pigeon's milk, a nutritious creamy substance produced in a special pouch in the throat of the pigeon called the crop. Hawks and owls bring rabbits or mice to the nest and feed them to the young in bits.

How often are birds fed? With an instrument called an itograph scientists have been able to answer this question accurately. A little perch at the entrance to the nest is pressed down whenever the bird goes in or out, and in this way the number of visits is recorded. From such records we know that young owls are fed ten times a night. Baby robins are brought almost a hundred meals a day, while the house wren parents make more than two hundred trips a day to the nest with food.

Even though in a great many cases the female alone takes care of the eggs until they hatch, the male usually joins in to help feed the young. A returning male woodpecker parent waits on a twig while his partner is feeding the young. Other birds fly off together and come back at the same time, or the male bird may only hand over the food to the female, which passes it on to the young. The European sparrow hawk male does all the hunting and delivers the food to the female, which stays at the nest. The mother hawk tears the prey into small pieces before offering it to the nestlings. If the female for some reason disappears from the nest, the male brings the food, but does not tear it up and offer it to the young. The young ones may cry for food, but the male hawk is unable to take on the female's role, and the young may die in the midst of a plentiful supply of food.

Protection from Danger

How are young birds protected from danger? This behavior varies with the kind of bird. Many young songbirds crouch in the nest and do not move when they hear alarm calls of their parents. While the young are in the nest, parent song sparrows give a *tchunk* call at the approach of a person, cat, or dog, and the young respond by crouching. If they have left the nest, but are still being fed by the parents, the mother bird gives a *tik-tik-tik* call when something alarming is near, and the young respond with silence.

gull chick
crouching

Ground-nesting birds respond to alarm calls as soon as they
hatch from their egg. In fact, it has been shown that gull chicks,
which squeak while still inside the egg, will become silent
before hatching when the parent sounds an alarm call. A newborn gull chick crouches in the nest in response to this call;
a day or so later it leaves the nest during the alarm and
crouches some distance away in the sand. Its color is speckled

brownish gray, which makes it almost invisible against the color of the sand.

Young chickens run and hide under the nearest shelter when the mother hen gives a loud, long drawn-out scream upon seeing a hawk in the sky. The high-pitched scream of a mother turkey will make young turkeys dash to cover, pile in clumps one on top of the other, and stay absolutely still. When the predator is on the ground, there are different alarm calls that make the chicks stop and freeze in their tracks or the turkey poults creep away in all directions.

If a duck is a surface feeder like a mallard, the mother gives low warning calls when she sights danger on the water. The young ducklings respond by gathering in a tight clump behind her. Either she will swim away rapidly with the ducklings following, or she will crouch with them among the water plants. Young diving ducks, like canvasbacks, escape an enemy by diving, swimming underwater, bobbing up for air, and then going under again, steadily moving away from the source of the disturbance.

Many female ducks react to an attack on their brood by flapping away from the ducklings. The female looks as if she is trying to rise and cannot. But she manages to stay ahead of her pursuer, and when she is far enough away she flies up into the air. Whenever the mother acts this way, the young rush away from her for the nearest cover or dive, depending on their kind. To us it appears that the mother is pretending to be wounded, but, of course, the bird does not consciously act such a role. She reacts this way automatically to an attack, and her action serves to call attention to her and away from from the young. Many other types of birds distract their enemies from their young with the same type of crippled fluttering movements. We do not know how this habit started among birds, but we do know that it has lasted in many species because it has helped the young birds to survive.

mother canvasback (distracting enemy)

ANIMALS AS PARENTS

Some mother birds defend their brood by attacking. The mother wild turkey hisses, runs, and jumps toward the intruder with wings beating the air and claws extended. A mother goose hisses and a father goose will threaten an enemy away with hisses and upraised wings too.

In spite of all the careful attention birds give to their eggs and young, there is a great loss of life among young birds. Floods drown some. Rain and windstorms and cold take a toll. The young birds may starve from lack of food or be eaten by other animals. The parent birds may be killed and the young ones then left without protection. Many birds die from eating insects containing insecticides. Only five to twenty percent of eggs laid produce young that grow up to be adult birds capable of breeding.

The few birds that survive grow up to adulthood in a relatively short time. Young robins become adult-sized in a month. At six weeks young gulls are full-grown and able to fly into the air and join the other gulls of the colony. A duck family remains together for about two months until the young can fly.

Four

Mammals
as
Parents

Mammals, the warm-blooded animals that have hair or fur, have a built-in way of feeding their young. They have special mammary glands that enlarge before the birth and secrete milk, a nourishing well-balanced food on which the young ones can survive till they are able to take solid food. The young are born alive after developing inside the body of the mother, but they are in widely different states of development at birth.

Just as some birds can run about on the first day of hatching, so there are mammals that can stand up and move shortly after birth. And there are also helpless ones that are born naked, blind, and deaf.

Ready to Move

The large grazing mammals, which live in herds and lead a shifting life in their search for the plant food they live on, generally have young that are able to stand up and move shortly after birth. These newborn young have hair; their eyes are open; and they are usually born large and long-legged.

Newborn goats and lambs rise on their wobbly legs in less than a half hour after birth. Within an hour the young manage to find a nipple on the body of the mother from which they can get milk. Sheep and goat mothers normally permit only their own young to nurse and reject strangers by moving away or butting them away. This early attachment is formed in the first few hours after birth. Experimenters have shown that immediately after giving birth a mother goat or sheep will accept any young kid or lamb, but within a few hours such an attachment is formed to her own young that she will reject any others presented to her. The mother goat and sheep will even reject her own offspring if they have been taken from her at birth and kept away for more than two to three

goat mother rejecting young not her own

hours. These first few hours represent a critical period during which the mother develops a social bond to her young. In a way the response is like imprinting among birds, for both are early experiences that produce long-lasting effects.

Young lambs stay close to their mother. They run along at her side and go to her to suckle milk for several months. The habit of following their mother persists through adulthood. Adult female sheep still follow their mother after their own lambs are born. Since each female tends to follow its mother, the lamb becomes part of a flock in which the oldest female is the leader.

If a young lamb is rejected by its mother, it is usually fed on a bottle. The person who supplies the bottle becomes the substitute mother. One such orphan was put in the field with other sheep and was butted away by the mother sheep it approached. After this experience the orphan lamb stayed away from the others and frequently followed the person who fed it milk from the bottle. In the poem that begins "Mary had a little lamb" we can see why "everywhere that Mary went the lamb was sure to go" if Mary was the one who fed the lamb milk from a bottle. In any case, a lamb that is rejected by its mother or removed from her at an early period of its life has an entirely different life history later on.

Ready to Swim

At the Marineland Research Laboratories in Florida porpoises (often called dolphins) have been watched through the portholes of a large seventy-five foot circular tank. For the first time it was possible to see the birth and early life of an infant porpoise.

Porpoises, like whales, are mammals that live underwater. Although they resemble fish, they breathe air and nurse their young. A baby porpoise is born underwater, and its birth creates a great deal of excitement in the tank. The other porpoises gather around the female giving birth and keep up a clamor of whistles and other sounds until the infant is born.

The baby weighs about twenty-five pounds and is almost a yard long. Within seconds after birth it surfaces for air. It can see, hear, whistle, and answer its mother's whistling calls. It can swim alongside its mother and keep up with her from the time it is born. If a newborn porpoise couldn't do these things, it would be separated quickly from its mother in the open sea and would not survive for long.

A few hours after birth the newborn porpoise begins to suck milk. Long periods of nursing are impossible for an infant that can rarely spend more than thirty seconds underwater without air. It is not surprising then to find that the mother porpoise has an adaptation that enables her to squirt enough milk for one feeding into the baby's mouth in a matter of seconds. The milk collects in large channels in her mammary glands, and when the infant grasps a nipple, the mother can contract muscles that force the milk out.

The newborn porpoise remains close to its mother during the first few months, the usual position being next to her top fin. If it strays more than ten feet away, the mother swims toward it and guides it close to her again. If an intruder gets too close to the infant, the mother claps

mother porpoise and young

her jaws and may even slap the enemy with her flukes. The infant is allowed to play with familiar objects in the tank, but it is steered away from any unfamiliar things. After six weeks the young porpoise begins to swim away from its mother regularly and to join other porpoises in play. But it goes back to its mother to rest.

After twelve months the young porpoises eat fish more and more, but they continue to nurse until they are about one and a half years old. The close relationship between the mother and her young may persist beyond this time and may even go on for years. Porpoises as much as four to six years old have been known to seek their mother's company when tired or alarmed. One pregnant female sought her mother's company and stayed with her most of the time during her entire pregnancy. Then, after the birth of the infant porpoise, grandmother and mother swam together with the infant between them, and the two adults guarded the young one throughout the first days of its life!

Helpless Young

Some mammals are born blind, deaf, and barely able to crawl. Newly born puppies have eyes and ears closed to the world, but they can smell, taste, and touch. Within minutes after birth they manage to locate the source of the milk supply — a nipple on their mother's body — and they begin to suck milk. For the first two weeks the puppies are in close contact with the mother. Actually she scarcely leaves them the first nine days. But from the second week on she leaves them more and more often.

At two weeks the puppies begin to open their eyes, and by the end of the third week they can hear. They can also walk and can take some solid food, for their first teeth appear then. They have grown to the point where they can see, hear, move around, and in general be responsive to their environment. Some scientists believe that the period from three to seven weeks is a critical period in a dog's

puppy refusing to follow on leash

life when it is most sensitive to the formation of social relationships. At this time it is easiest for an experimenter in a laboratory to make social contact with a puppy. A puppy that has had contact with people during this period later follows a person on a leash without any trouble. A puppy that has had no contact with people at this same period shows fear and refuses to follow. Again early experience produces lasting effects. The best time then to buy a puppy and to form enduring social ties with it is when it is between three and seven weeks old.

During this period the puppy also forms social relationships with the other puppies in the litter. It plays and fights with them. If a dog has had such normal social exchange with the members of its litter, it remains friendly to dogs and is capable of teaming together with them in packs. One experimenter separated young dogs and raised them in isolation. When they were put back with their group-raised littermates, the dogs were at first very responsive, but later tended to withdraw from the others.

During the fourth week the mother begins to punish her pups by growling and snapping when they approach her to nurse. This behavior is the beginning of the weaning process, and by eight weeks the young puppy generally stops taking milk from its mother and depends more and more on solid food. It becomes an independent animal.

Scientists have asked, "What is the nature of the social attachment of dogs to people?" Does it depend only on the fact that a person gives the dog food? An experiment was done to try to answer this question. Two groups of cocker-spaniel puppies were raised in two different ways. One group was fed by hand and the other group by machine. But both groups were played with for an equal time by the person in charge of the experiment. The results showed that even those fed by machine became attached to the experimenter. Food was not the main basis of the socialization process.

Cats are not social like dogs. They tend to live a solitary life. But some kittens grow up to be good house pets and show great attachment to people while others become wild, avoiding people and other cats. Why do these differences occur? Studies have shown that what happens to a kitten during the weeks after it is born largely determines the kind of cat it will be. In an experiment kittens were removed from their mother at two, six, and twelve weeks of age and reared in identical living cages after that. When they grew up to be adults they behaved very differently. Those

anxious cat

normal cat

that were separated from the mother at two weeks were the most anxious and disturbed in situations new to them and the slowest to learn simple feeding routines. Throughout their life they were suspicious, fearful, and aggressive in their behavior toward other cats. The ones that were separated at six weeks, the time of normal weaning, and at twelve weeks, were more successful in food competitions and, in general, much more normal in their behavior. So again infantile experience has been found to be highly important.

Rats are unpleasant creatures to most of us. But as laboratory animals rats are invaluable, for they do not take up much room and they are easy to care for. In the course of experiments done with these animals, some were kept in separate nests and the environment was carefully controlled for temperature, humidity, light, and other factors. These rats were not handled at all. They were compared to another group of rats that were handled every day by the experimenter for a brief period of time. The interesting thing was that the unhandled rats turned out to be peculiar when tested as adults. During the tests they were put in unfamiliar surroundings, and their reactions were noted. They cowered in a corner or crept around timidly. The handled rats acted normally and freely explored the strange place.

Other experiments have shown that a rat that is kept isolated from other rats in its early life is a nervous, aggressive animal with a pronounced tendency to bite. In fact, it is impossible to handle these rats as others are handled. The same kind of rats kept in pairs in the cages for the same amount of time were found to be normal in behavior.

More and more evidence is accumulating indicating that young mammals of many species are extremely sensitive during their infancy.

Five

Mother Love Among Monkeys and Apes

An infant monkey or ape is born into a society. Many monkeys and apes live in groups consisting of males, females, and their young.

The newborn monkey or ape clings to its mother or is carried by her as she moves around. It sucks milk from her mammary glands when it is hungry. The mother cleans her infant and protects it from other members of the group and from enemies. The infant stays with its mother for a long time, varying from a number of months to a few

years. As it grows, it spends more and more time playing with other infants and young apes. From its constant
contact with its mother and with other group members it
learns the habits and social relationships of the society it was
born into.

Baboons

Baboons are monkeys that spend most of their time on the
ground. We know what the life of a newborn baboon is like,
because scientists have watched baboons going about their
daily lives in Kenya, Africa. The animals did not seem to
be disturbed by automobiles, so most of the material was
gathered while the scientists remained inside a Land Rover
jeep within a few yards of them. Baboons live in troops
that may consist of as few as ten or as many as two hundred,
and they may travel three miles in a day. Observations were
relatively easy to make, because the troops could be followed
on wheels. The scientists watched them for twelve hundred
hours and recorded what they saw by dictating into a
portable tape recorder. They also took photographs and
movies.

The newborn baboon is the center of social attraction. All
the members of the troop try to get close to the babies, so a
mother and her infant are always surrounded by other

baboons. A few older males of the group dominate all other troop members, and as soon as the infant is born the mother moves close to these dominant males, which protect her from other members of the group and from outside enemies.

The newborn can hold onto its mother a few hours after it is born. While it clings to the hair on her abdomen, the mother can move along with the troop. When the troop rests, the baby is allowed to nurse. The mother spends a great deal of time grooming the baby. She explores its fur and picks out any foreign matter as well as parasites. When the baby is restless, she smacks her lips and this sound has a quieting effect on it just as a human mother's singing soothes her infant. Although other adult males and females are always crowding around her, she does not let anyone touch the infant for one week after it is born. Then she may allow the baboons that sit beside her to touch it briefly.

At the end of the first month the infant takes a few steps away from its mother. If two mothers are sitting close by, their infants move toward each other, quickly touch, and run right back to their mother. Most of the infants are born together during the rainy season, so there are plenty of play-mates for them.

mother baboon carrying young

After two months the infant often rides the female's back, first clinging to her fur, and then sitting up like a jockey riding a horse. By six months it has tried some solid food. As it grows, the infant spends more and more time away from its mother playing with other youngsters. By the age of ten months it plays most of the day. The older males watch these play groups. If the playing gets too rough, an adult male stares at the group and grunts softly, and this signal stops the roughhouse immediately.

At this time the mother begins to brush her infant away

77

from her breast when it tries to nurse. Usually it returns to sleep with its mother at nightfall. At fifteen months the baby is weaned from its mother, and the ties between them are weak. When it is two years old, the mother has a new baby. The young baboon now has strong ties to other members of the troop and is fully capable of feeding itself and taking its place in baboon society.

Howling Monkeys

Howling monkeys are tree-living monkeys that live in the jungles of Central and South America. It is interesting to see how life in the treetops affects the infant monkey. As in baboon society, the closest ties in the group are between the female and her baby. The infant clings to its mother's body all the time and nurses when hungry. The mother seems to have no trouble at all climbing high up in the trees with the tiny baby clinging to her. Once in a while there is an accident, and a baby falls to the ground. It cries in a high-pitched voice, and usually the mother leaps down to pick up the infant and climb back up into the trees. When it is two weeks old, it starts to ride on its mother's back. After a few weeks the baby begins to leave its mother and explore the leaves and branches around her while she rests. By one month of age its movements are well-coordinated, and it wanders as much as ten feet from its mother. As it grows it plays more and more with other young ones. Chasing through the trees, wrestling, and hanging by its tail become part of its everyday activities.

The howling-monkey clan moves through the trees feeding on fruit and leaves. Some routes are difficult, and mother howlers have often been seen helping their young ones across such places by holding one tree with their hands and the other with their feet, thus forming a bridge over which the infant can cross. Although it starts to eat leaves and fruits at the age of one month, the infant continues to nurse until it is one and a half to two years of age. Gradually it loses its close attachments to its mother and participates in the social life of the howling-monkey clan.

The relationship between infant monkeys and their mother seems to be pretty much the same whether they live in the trees or on the ground. But even these wonderful studies of monkey life in the wild do not tell us as much about the infant-mother relationship as recent exciting new information from laboratories where experiments are being carried on with rhesus monkeys. These monkeys are the most common ones in Asia.

At the University of Wisconsin a breeding colony of rhesus monkeys has been used to investigate problems of growth and learning. The experiments required controlled conditions—that is, the environment had to be the same for all the monkeys before they were given special tests. Baby monkeys were removed from their mother a few hours after birth and put into wire cages in a monkey nursery. The infant monkeys were treated like human babies. They were fed milk in bottles. They were given vitamins, iron, antibiotics when they needed them, and gradually were shifted to solid food. These bottle-fed babies were healthier and heavier than those raised by their own mother.

Rhesus Monkeys

During these studies it was noticed that the baby monkeys were very much attached to the cloth pad used to cover the floor of the cage. The baby monkeys showed great distress when the pads were removed once a day for cleaning purposes. They clung to the pad and acted as some human babies do if you try to separate them from their favorite blanket or cuddly toy.

This behavior led to the idea that part of the infant's attachment to its mother might depend upon contact with her body. So the experimenters, Dr. Harry E. Harlow and Margaret K. Harlow, built two kinds of artificial mothers. One was a wire cylinder with a wooden head. The other was a wire cylinder covered by a layer of terry cloth. Eight infant monkeys were put into separate cages each with a cloth mother and a wire mother. Milk was supplied by nursing bottles protruding from the chest area of the models. In four cages only the cloth mothers supplied milk. In the other four cages only the wire mothers supplied it. The results showed that though the monkeys in the two groups drank the same amount of milk, all the infants spent most of their time holding and hugging their soft terry-cloth mothers, even when they had to nurse from the wire mother. These experiments answered an important question. What ties an infant monkey to its mother is not so much that she is a source of food, but that her body offers a source of contact comfort.

In frightening situations the infants showed that they could find security in the presence of their cloth mothers. When a toy mechanical Teddy bear beating a drum was moved toward an infant monkey, the infant rushed to its cloth mother rather than to its wire one. After it had rubbed against her and calmed down, it turned and looked at the strange object. The infants were subjected to other frightening situations. They were put into a room that was much larger than their usual cage and presented with strange objects. A typical infant then rushed to its cloth mother and,

81

after a while, left it to explore the new objects. If the cloth mother were not in the cage, the infant threw itself down on the floor and screamed. The wire mother was no comfort at all.

The cloth mother seemed to be ideal. It was never angry or cross, and it was available at all times for the infant to climb on. But strange things began to show up when these infant monkeys that had never known a real monkey mother grew up. These monkeys proved to be peculiar. They sat in their cages and stared into space or rocked back and forth or bit themselves—a type of behavior found among human patients in mental institutions! Most of these monkeys did not mate even when they were given chances to do so. Only a few females did mate, and when they became mothers they acted abnormally. Normal mothers clasp their baby tightly, nurse it, and protect it from any intruder that comes near. These mothers rejected their infant, brushed it off, and made nursing difficult or impossible for it. Something was missing in the artificial mothers, or perhaps another factor entered into the situation. Besides not having real mothers, these infant monkeys had not had any chance to play with other baby monkeys for the first three years of their life. They were in cages where they could see, hear, and communicate with other babies, but they could not

infant rhesus monkey clinging to cloth mother

touch them or play with them the way normal monkeys play with each other in the wild.

How important was this factor? Could infant monkeys be separated from their mother and yet grow up normally if they were given a chance to be with other infants during the first six months of their life?

To test this possibility the following experiment was done. Four monkeys were raised in cages with their own monkey mother and compared with four monkey infants raised by a cloth mother. Sixteen days after they were born, each infant monkey was permitted to spend two hours a day in a playroom with a companion. The mother-raised infants played together much sooner and in a much livelier way than the ones raised by artificial mothers. But at the end of their second year the early differences disappeared, and the artificially mothered animals were almost normal. At present all we can say is that play with other infants seems to make up for the lack of a real mother.

New experiments always raise new questions that have to be answered by further experiments, and so the work with rhesus monkeys goes on.

Gorillas and Chimpanzees

Monkeys belong to a group of mammals called *primates.*

85

The manlike apes and man himself belong in this group. Since the manlike apes are our closest relatives, the details of their family life are especially interesting to us.

Not too much was known about the life of infant gorillas until a young scientist and his wife set out in 1959 on a two-year expedition to find out what they could about the family life of gorillas that live in the mountains of Africa. After a long survey of gorilla country, they selected the cool open forests of the Virunga Mountains in Albert National Park in the Congo.

Some early explorers in Africa had described the gorilla as a ferocious, ill-tempered beast dangerous to man. But other work had shown that gorillas were approachable and could be studied without fear of attack. Instead of starting out with a large party of gunbearers, camera carriers, trackers, and porters as others had done before them, these researchers decided to go alone and unarmed. In plain sight of the gorillas they approached them slowly to within a distance of about one hundred feet. If the gorillas moved away, they would not follow, for gorillas are most likely to attack if pursued. Hour after hour George B. Schaller, and sometimes his wife, sat in the low branches of a tree and watched the gorillas as they ate, rested, played, and slept. The gorillas got used to his sitting near them and sometimes even got as close as twelve feet to have a closer look at him. After a while Schaller could distinguish the members of the group. Gorillas live in troops of from two to thirty animals. Usually there are twice as many females as males and an assortment of young ones.

An infant gorilla weighs only three to four pounds when it is born. It cannot hold on to its mother by itself, so the mother gorilla clasps it tightly and carries it with one arm against her chest as she walks on three limbs. She likes to sit near the dominant, or boss male of the troop. He is the one who leads the others, determining their time of rising, somewhere between 6 to 8 A.M., the way to travel, the length of the feeding and resting periods, and the time and place to build nests of branches and leaves for the night. Often he plays with the infants and lets them climb all over him and even ride on his back.

By three months the young infant gorilla can ride on the back of its mother when the troop moves. The mother protects the baby at all times. Until it is four to five months old, it is not allowed to move more than ten feet away from her. But by five months the infant crawls away far enough to play with other gorilla babies. By six to seven months it climbs by itself and toddles after its mother if not being carried on her back. By eight months, although it is still getting milk from its mother, most of its nourishment comes from the plants that adult gorillas eat. Gorillas eat about twenty-five different kinds of plants, and the young ones seem to learn which are good to eat by watching other group members and by trying different plants themselves. Soon they are ripping, shredding, and tearing roots, stems, leaves, and bark like the others.

By the time the young gorilla is a year old, it is playing with other youngsters a great deal of the time, wrestling and chasing through the trees. Ties between baby and mother loosen. When it is a year and a half old it stops nursing. By two and a half years it is nearly independent, but is still sleeping with its mother at night. When it is three to four years old, its mother generally has a new baby, and now the young gorilla is really on its own except that it has become integrated into the group life of its kind.

Chimpanzees are thought to be the smartest of the apes. They are easily trained and learn things easily. And they can even solve certain simple problems. Although they spend much more time in the trees than gorillas do, they take care of their infants in much the same way. Chimpanzee infants stay with their mother for five or six years instead of three to four years as gorillas do. Even up to the age of sexual maturity (eight or nine years) the chimpanzee young

gorilla mother carrying infant

chimpanzee mother and infant

are seldom let out of sight by their mother. This constant and long control of the young by the mother is an essential part of chimpanzee social life.

The Role of Early Experience

The whole subject of the role of early experience in the life of animals is fascinating. The first few hours after a lamb or kid is born determines its future, for it is then that the mother sheep or goat forms her attachment to her offspring. The first days after a duck, goose, turkey, or chicken hatches out of its egg are tremendously important. The environment at this early age can have widespread effects on its later life. The early experience of dogs, rats, and cats produces effects that can last a lifetime. Baby monkeys need their mother or at least other baby monkeys in infancy in order to grow up to be normal monkeys.

If early experience is so important in the life of these animals, what role does it play in the life of human infants? We do not know enough about this subject, for one cannot experiment with babies. However, the studies on animals have given scientists some insight into factors that may be important in this connection. Newborn babies are being observed in hospitals with certain questions in mind. Is it better for a baby to be with its mother as soon as possible after it is born? Or is it better for the baby to be taken care of by nurses in a separate nursery room? Perhaps human babies are not as sensitive to their surroundings right after birth, for they grow very slowly compared to other animals. The environment may have a much greater effect on them later when they are a few months old. Further research on child development in the light of animal studies may help us to identify those experiences most beneficial to the future life of human beings.

Suggestions
for
Further
Reading

(P) means paperback

Armstrong, Edward A., *The Way Birds Live*. London: Lindsay Drummond Ltd., 1943.

Burton, Maurice, *Infancy in Animals*. New York: Roy Publishers, 1956.

Carrington, Richard, *The Mammals*. New York: Life Nature Library, Time, Inc., 1964.

Gramet, Charles, *Reproduction and Sex in Animal Life*. New York: Abelard-Schuman, 1962.

Heinroth, Oscar and Katharina, *The Birds*. Ann Arbor: University of Michigan Press, 1958 (P).

ANIMALS AS PARENTS

Lanham, Urlesf M., *The Fishes*. New York: Columbia University Press, 1962.

McClung, Robert M., *All About Animals and Their Young*. New York: Random House, 1958.

Noble, Ruth C., *Nature of the Beast*. New York: Doubleday, 1945.

Ommanney, Francis D., *The Fishes*. New York: Life Nature Library, Time, Inc., 1963.

Peterson, Roger T., *The Birds*. New York: Life Nature Library, Time, Inc., 1963.

Schaller, George B., *The Year of the Gorilla*. Chicago: University of Chicago Press, 1964.

Selsam, Millicent E., *How Animals Live Together*. New York: William Morrow and Company, 1963.

Selsam, Millicent E., *The Courtship of Animals*. New York: William Morrow and Company, 1964.

Southwick, Charles H., *Primate Social Behavior*. New York: D. Van Nostrand and Company, 1963 (P).

Tinbergen, Nikolaas, *The Herring Gull's World*. New York: Basic Books, 1961.

Tinbergen, Nikolaas, *Social Behavior in Animals*. New York: John Wiley & Sons, 1953.

Welty, Joel, *The Life of Birds*. New York: Alfred A. Knopf, 1963.

Zeichner, Irving, *How Life Goes On*. New York: Prentice-Hall, Inc., 1960.

Magazines like *Scientific American, Natural History,* and *Audubon Magazine* often have articles on animal parent-infant relations.

Index

Indicates illustrations